This
Book
Belongs
To _____

Grolier Enterprises Inc.
SHERMAN TURNPIKE, DANBURY, CONNECTICUT 06816

Book Club Edition

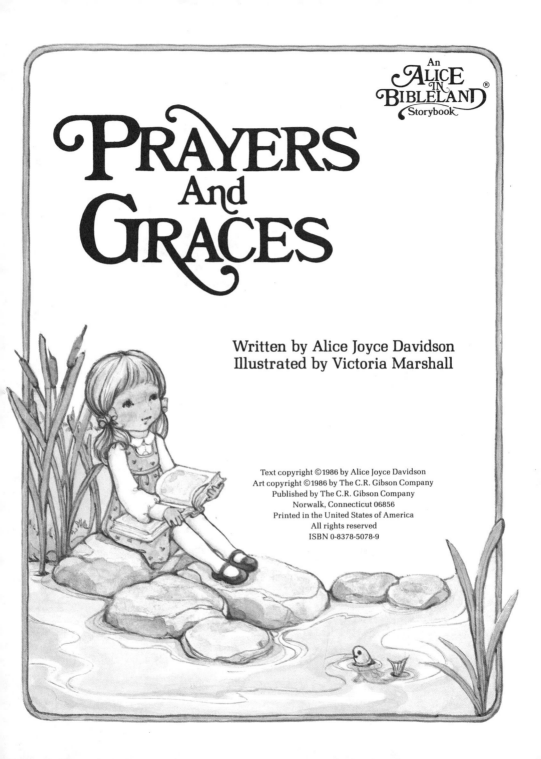

An **ALICE IN BIBLELAND** ® Storybook

PRAYERS And GRACES

Written by Alice Joyce Davidson
Illustrated by Victoria Marshall

Text copyright ©1986 by Alice Joyce Davidson
Art copyright ©1986 by The C.R. Gibson Company
Published by The C.R. Gibson Company
Norwalk, Connecticut 06856
Printed in the United States of America
ISBN 0-8378-5078-9

A little girl named Alice
Has a Bible all her own.
It tells about God's glory
And all the love He's shown.

Her little Bible helps her
As she learns, and works and plays.
Its words of wisdom guide her, too,
Every time she prays.

Because she likes to share things,
Alice thought the thing to do

Was to write her prayers and graces down
And share them all with you.

Ask, and it shall be given you.
Matthew 7:7

Dear Lord, I know You're busy
With a million things to do,
But, please, can You take time to hear
My special prayers to You?

I've prayers to ask Your guidance,
And prayers of grace, as well.
All my prayers are filled with love—
Much more than words can tell!
Amen

My voice shalt thou hear
in the morning, O Lord.

Psalms 5:3

It's morning time,
        So thank You, Lord,
For things to do
        And things to see.
It's morning time,
        And, Lord, I feel
The sunshine of
        Your love for me!

Amen

The Lord bless thee, and keep thee.

Numbers 6:24

Dear Lord I pray
As day is done,
Look down upon
Your little one.
Please stay with me
Throughout the night,
And keep me safe
Till morning's light.

Amen

Be not dismayed; for I am thy God:
I will strengthen thee.

Isaiah 41:10

Dear Lord,
I feel a bit uncertain.
I've something new to do.
Please guide my way
Throughout the day
And keep me close to You.

Amen

He careth for you.
1 Peter 5:7

Please help me to feel better, Lord;
Please hear my little prayer.
Hold me in Your arms, Lord;
Let me feel Your loving care.

Amen

Two are better than one.
Ecclesiastes 4:9

Dear Lord,
Thank You for my special friend
To share with and to love.
A good friend is a treasure
And a blessing from above.

Amen

Her children arise up,
and call her blessed.
Proverbs 31:28

Dear Lord,
    You've blessed me with a mother
Who's dear in every way.
    I pray that You will bless her, too,
With good things every day.

Amen

Hear the instruction of thy father.

Proverbs 1:8

Dear God,
    Fathers are for being with,
For learning from, for talking with,
    Fathers are for seeing with,
For sharing, and for walking with,
    Fathers are just everything
That's wonderful and fine.
    Thank You, God, for fathers—
Especially for MINE!

                              Amen

Honour thy father and thy mother.

Exodus 20:12

Dear Lord, I love my parents.
Please guide me from above
And teach me all the many ways
That I can show my love.

Amen

Thy father and thy mother shall be glad.

Proverbs 23:25

Dear Lord,
I love my parents,
Please guide me so I'll be
So very good that both of them
Will be real proud of me.

Amen

I am come that they might have life,
and that they might have it
more abundantly.

John 10:10

Dear Lord,
Bless this home and all who live here,
Everyone who visits, too.
May it be a place of gladness
Every day the whole year through.

Amen

The earth is full of
the goodness of the Lord.
Psalms 33:5

Birds and bees and shady trees,
Tall grass and secret places,
Dandelions to sniff and blow,
And pretty pansy faces,
Cherries, berries, plums and pears,
Delicious things to eat—
The earth is full of Your good things,
Your gifts are mighty sweet!

Amen

The flowers appear on the earth;
the time of the singing of birds is come.

Song of Solomon 2:12

Did You see the flowers dancing?
Did You hear the robin sing?
They're happy, just as I am, God,
And full of thanks for spring!

Amen

Thou hast made summer.
Psalms 74:17

Summer showers, butterflies,
Fluffy clouds, and bright blue skies,
New adventures, friends and fun,
Swimming, playing in the sun,
Flowers blooming, shady trees—
Thank You, God, for all of these!

Amen

Thou crownest the year with thy goodness.

Psalms 65:11

Thank You, God, for autumn,
A season of good cheer,
An apple-crunching,
Popcorn-munching,
Happy time of year.
And as we pick the harvest,
I feel Your presence near.

Amen

Awake, O north wind.
Song of Solomon 4:16

Thank You, God, for winter,
A restful time of year.
The days are short, the nights are long.
The air is crisp and clear.
And in this quiet restful time,
I feel Your presence near.

Amen

O sing unto the Lord a new song.

Psalms 98:1

Snowflakes, flowers,
Rainbows, showers—
Every season through—
I find new things to sing about
Dear Lord in praise of YOU!

Amen

A feast is made for laughter.
Ecclesiastes 10:19

Dear God,
We thank You for this gathering
And for our joyful mood.
We ask You, Lord, to bless us
As we share Your gift of food.
Amen

Thou hast granted me life and favour.

Job 10:12

Dear God,
Thank You for this happy day,
This day that marks my birth,
And thank You, too, for giving me
A good life on this earth.

Amen

Walk worthy of the vocation
wherewith ye are called.
Ephesians 4:1

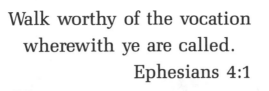

Dear Lord,
Take my lips and put on them
The kindest words to say.
Take my hands and make them strong
To do Your work today.
Take my feet and guide them, Lord,
To always walk Your way.

Amen

Be ye kind one to another.
Ephesians 4:32

I'm sorry, Lord, for acting
The way I did today.
I feel bad when I hurt someone
By things I do or say.
I pray that You will help me, Lord.
Please lead me in Your way.

Amen

Love thy neighbour as thyself.
Romans 13:9

Dear God,
Please help me to be kind and sweet
To folks I know and those I meet,
To do for others happily
Those things that I'd like done for me!
Amen

I am with you always.
Matthew 28:20

Dear Lord,
You're always there to guide me,
To teach me right from wrong.
Whatever path I travel,
I'm glad that You're along.

Amen

The nations shall bless themselves
in him.

Jeremiah 4:2

Bless my country, Lord, I pray
With everything that's good
So we may share Your loving gifts
In peace and brotherhood.

Amen

God blessed the seventh day,
and sanctified it.

Genesis 2:3

Dear God,
Thank You for this Sabbath day,
A holy day of rest,
A day to praise Your name with prayer
And feel especially blessed.

Amen

He filled their houses with good things.

Job 22:18

Dear Lord,
Thank You for this gift of food
You've placed upon our table,
And help us all to do Your work
In any way we're able.

Amen

Consider the wondrous works of God.

Job 37:14

Dear God,
We thank You for the meal we've had,
And want to thank You, too,
For all the many gifts of love
We daily get from YOU.

Amen

We love him, because he first loved us.

1 John 4:19

I love You, God,
  I hope You know it
By the ways
  I try to show it.

I love You, God,
  And I know, too,
I have the gift
  Of love from YOU!
    Amen

My lips shall praise thee.
Psalms 63:3

Praise our Father up above.
Praise Him for His care and love.
Praise Him for dear families,
For sun, for rain, for fruiting trees.
Praise Him for His guiding light,
For being with us day and night.
For every gift of His we share,
Sing His praises with a prayer!

Amen